I Can Do It!

I Can Tie My Shoes

By Meg Gaertner

level 1 little blue readers

www.littlebluehousebooks.com

Little Blue House is distributed by North Star Editions:
sales@northstareditions.com | 888-417-0195

Produced for Little Blue House by Red Line Editorial.

Photographs ©: Shutterstock Images cover, 7, 8–9, 10–11, 12–13, 15, 16–17, 19, 21, 22–23, 24 (top left), 24 (top right), 24 (bottom left), 24 (bottom right); iStockphoto, 4

Library of Congress Control Number: 2022901676

ISBN
978-1-64619-582-4 (hardcover)
978-1-64619-609-8 (paperback)
978-1-64619-662-3 (ebook pdf)
978-1-64619-636-4 (hosted ebook)

Printed in the United States of America
Mankato, MN
082022

About the Author

Meg Gaertner enjoys reading, writing, dancing, and being outside. She lives in Minnesota.

Table of Contents

mom
shoe

I Can Tie My Shoes

I can tie my shoes.

I tie my shoes with my mom.

I can tie my shoes.
I tie my shoes with
my dad.

dad

I can tie my shoes.
I tie my shoes with
my grandma.

grandma

I can tie my shoes.
I tie my shoes with
my grandpa.

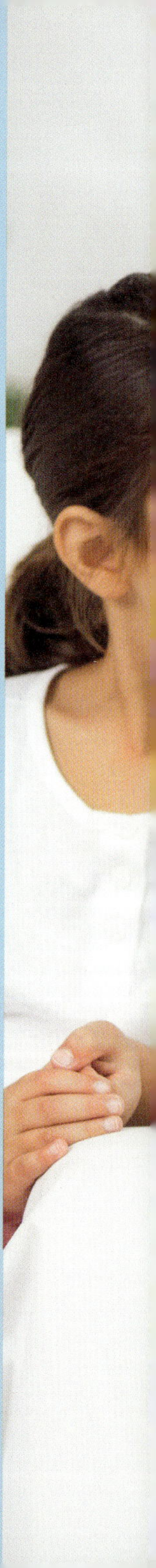

grandpa

I can tie my shoes.
I tie my shoes with
my sister.

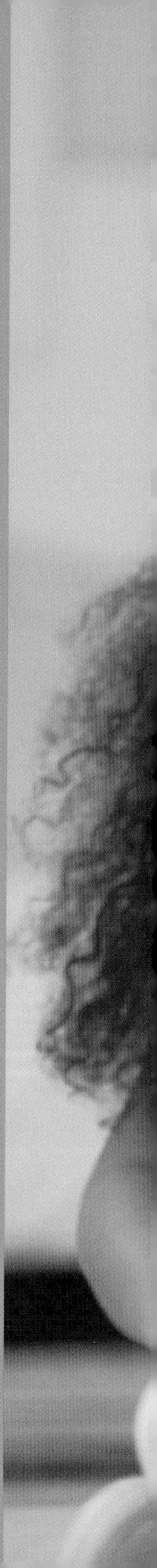

sister

I can tie my shoes.
I tie my shoes with
my brother.

brother

I can tie my shoes.
I tie my shoes with
my friend.

friend

I can tie my shoes.
I tie my shoes with
my teacher.

teacher

I can tie my shoes.

I tie my shoes by myself.

I can tie my shoes.
I tie my shoes with
my dog.

dog

Glossary

dog

grandpa

grandma

teacher

Index